When the Spirit Comes Upon You

Nine days of reflections and prayers for the gifts of the Holy Spirit
Series I

Fr. Emmanuel Okami

FLOREAT SYSTEMS PUBLICATIONS
BENIN CITY

ISBN: 979-865-179-294-8

IMPRIMATUR
Bishop Ayo Maria Atoyebi, OP
Bishop Emeritus of Ilorin Diocese, Nigeria

NIHIL OBSTAT
Very Rev. Fr. Stephen Audu
Ilorin Diocese,

★★★★★

EDITOR
Lisa Timms
Customer Manager, Global Operations,
British Airways Plc.
Our Lady of Peace Parish, Burnham, UK.

★★★★★

COVER ART
Senux Media
www.senuxmedia.com

Floreat Systems Press
www.floreatsystem.com.ng

★★★★★

Printed by:
Floreat Systems, Catholic Archdiocese of Benin Printing Press
30, Airport Road, Benin City, Edo State, Nigeria

Dedicated in
Thanksgiving to God

For

Restoring the health of
Sam A.

FOREWORD

In the words of an Orthodox bishop, '"Without the Holy Spirit, God is far away, Christ stays in the past, the Gospel is a dead letter, the Church is simply an organisation, authority a matter of domination, mission a matter of propaganda, liturgy no more than an evocation, Christian living a slave morality."

No Christian can live a fulfilled and fruitful life without the Holy Spirit. The Holy Spirit resurrects the 'dead and dry bones' and brings them to life.

Not only does Fr. Emmanuel's book, *When the Spirit Comes Upon You*, help the reader to grow in the life of the Holy Spirit, it also enables them to live in freedom, as a child of God. It further opens the eyes of their heart to the recognition that the Gospel is the power of life. It is simple and easy to read but deep in spiritual nourishment, as it explains the Seven Gifts of the Holy Spirit.

I am confident that those who have the privilege of reading this book and the prayer reflections on the Seven Gifts of the Holy Spirit, will find an enrichment, that may bring about in their lives a new experience of Pentecost.

Fr. William Pius Amoako
Northampton Diocese, UK and Sion Community for Evangelism

*****

Reviews

In the Nicene creed of the Church we profess our faith:

"Et in Spiritum Sanctum, Dominum et vivificantem, qui ex Patre Filioque procedit. Qui cum Patre et Filio simul adoratur et conglorificatur: qui locutus est per prophetas."

" ...And in the Holy Spirit, the Lord, the giver of life, who proceeds from the Father and the Son, who with the Father and the Son is adored and glorified, who has spoken through the prophets".

This summarises the person of the Holy Spirit, and His work. The importance of the Holy Spirit cannot be overemphasised in the life of every child of God; in fact, He is the one that confirms our identity and the seal of God's ownership on our lives (cf. Romans 8:15-16, Ephesians 1:13b-14).

Fr. Emmanuel has emphasized the PERSONHOOD of the Holy Spirit, and this is very key to any meaningful relationship with Him. He is the giver of life. He vivifies everything; our prayer lives (Romans 8:26), and our relationship with God and humanity. He gives life to our worship; hence we are called to worship "in Spirit and in truth." Without the Holy Spirit, our worship, prayers, and religious practices would be boring routines, empty verbosity and fruitless endeavours.

Fr. Emmanuel is as a great teacher of the truths of the Gospel, and a powerful writer, inspired by the Holy Spirit, hence this book is in sync with his characteristic way of elucidating truths. In this book, Fr. Emmanuel not only talks of the Holy Spirit, he writes about the seven sanctifying gifts of the Spirit as mentioned in the Catechism of the Catholic Church. These are different to the "charismatic gifts" mentioned in 1st Corinthians chapters 12 and 14. These sanctifying gifts, work for our salvation, while the charismatic gifts build up the body of Christ. More importantly, Fr. Emmanuel brings out the Fruits of the Holy Spirit (Galatians 5:22ff); these are basic indices of measurement for Christians.

The practical approach of Fr. Emmanuel in this book is laudable, because many find it difficult to actually go through seminars like this gainfully, due to a lack of practical steps for achieving the goal. However, with prayers, copious examples and scriptural backings, Fr. Emmanuel teaches practical ways of receiving these gifts, how to use them, and how they work.

We must be really thirsty for Him (John 7:37-39) and we must ask our heavenly Father to give us His Spirit; He won't refuse us (Luke 11:13). As we prepare for the feast of the birth of the Church, Pentecost, let us make great use of this manual and really prepare to encounter the Paraclete. Pentecost should not be just a story; it is a living experience.

Come Holy Spirit, fill the hearts of the faithful...and enkindle in us the fire of your love.

Rev. Fr. Anthony Adeboyejo
Catholic institute of West Africa

*****

The book, *When the Spirit Comes Upon You*, has really helped me to better understand the actual spiritual meaning of the Gifts of the Holy spirit. As a Catholic I have learnt about them, but to date, I have failed to implement them in my life.

Fr. Emmanuel has explained, in a realistic way, how the Holy Spirit is an ever-present reality in our lives. This book is a nine-day reflective journey through the enumerated gifts of the Holy Spirit, supported by scripture and prayer, which shows how these gifts can have a significant impact in our lives. Whilst I was reading this book, I really felt a call to study and understand more about the Holy spirit's gifts. I strongly recommend this spiritual book, as I believe it will help anyone to develop their relationship with the Holy spirit.

Sharlotte Pires
Duty Customer Experience Manager, Transport for London,
Our Lady of Peace Church, Burnham, UK.

*****

The book, *When the Spirit Comes Upon You* by Rev. Fr. Emmanuel Okami, is a very reviving instrument to the readers and even to the writer. Many times, when reading the Word of God, we are taught a new lesson. It also re-germinates the world of God in us, so we are born as new children in Christ Jesus.
This book will always keep us in check of our Christianity today. I have no doubt in my mind that it is a blessing in our world of today.

Peter O. Nwokobia
Blessed Sacrament Catholic Church, Bronx, NY, USA.

*****

Fr. Emmanuel has been truly inspired and guided by the Holy Spirit in writing this book, *When the Spirit Comes Upon You,* which is simple and easy to read and meditate on during our daily spiritual journey. This book helped me to experience the tangible presence of the Holy Trinity.

Anxiously awaiting the follow up of Fr. Emmanuel's book.

Cedrica Lobo
Lead Administrator, NHS Slough
Our Lady of Peace Church, Burnham, UK

*****

WHEN THE SPIRIT COMES UPON YOU

*Nine days of reflection and prayers
for the Gifts of the
Holy Spirit*

Series 1

When the Spirit Comes Upon You

TABLE OF CONTENTS

*****

INTRODUCTION

The Holy Spirit is the least talked about amongst the three persons of the Holy Trinity; He is the least known, the least understood and the most misunderstood.

Some people do not even see the Holy Spirit as a Divine Person, but more as something like a force, an energy, a natural element like fire or wind. For many others, He is a ghost or simply a dove. People often confuse symbol or representation with the reality.

There are so many people who think that we have moved away from the era of the Holy Spirit; that it was an exclusive experience of the early Church as recorded in the Acts of the Apostles.

This book, *When the Spirit Comes Upon You*, is the first in a three series reflection on the Holy Spirit. This first series focuses on the Seven Gifts of the Holy Spirit. Relying on Isaiah 11:1-3 and the tradition of the Church, the Catholic Catechism teaches that there are seven gifts of the Holy Spirit:

"The seven gifts of the Holy Spirit are wisdom, understanding, counsel, fortitude, knowledge, piety, and fear of the Lord. They belong in their fullness to Christ, Son of David. They complete and perfect the virtues of those who receive them. They make the faithful docile in readily obeying divine inspirations." CCC 1831.

This list does not in any way exhaust the gifts of the Holy Spirit. The Holy Spirit touches our lives in a variety of ways too numerous to be enumerated.

This particular series takes us through a nine-day journey of reflection on and praying for these enumerated gifts of the Holy Spirit.

The second series of this book will take us through some reflections and prayers for the fruits of the Holy Spirit as listed in Galatians 5:22.

The third series shall reflect on the various manifestations of the Holy Spirit, as we have it written in 1 Corinthians 12:8-10 and also in Romans 12:6-8, Ephesians 4:11, and 1 Peter 4:10-11.

My vision is to help the faithful broaden their understanding and awareness of the third person of the Holy Trinity, the person of the Holy Spirit, known as the Paraclete, and His role in the life of a Christian.

I wish to affirm that the experience of the Holy Spirit is an ever-present reality; it is not something that has ceased. You and I could experience the Holy Spirit again and anew; we could be refilled, revived, re-awakened, re-energised, renewed and re-strengthened by the Holy Spirit.

At the end of the book, I have some prayers to the Holy Spirit, which are aimed at deepening our awareness of His presence and power, to nurture our intimacy with Him, so we may profit abundantly from this supernatural relationship.

It is my ardent wish that this book will serve as a guideline to a better understanding of the meaning and importance of the gifts of the Holy Spirit and help us to desire, pray and obtain them through faith.

It is my desire in good faith that this book will help someone, somewhere, to grow in intimacy with the Holy Spirit and receive what the Holy Spirit is willing to give.

Fr Emmanuel Okami
Word of Life Ministry, Milton Keynes, UK,
A Priest of Ilorin Diocese, Nigeria,
On Mission in Northampton Diocese, UK.

*****

Come, Holy Spirit. Spirit of truth, you are the reward of the saints, the comforter of souls, light in the darkness, riches to the poor, treasure to lovers, food for the hungry, comfort to those who are wandering; to sum up, you are the one in whom all treasures are contained. Come! As you descended upon Mary that the Word might become flesh, work in us through grace as you worked in her through nature and grace. Come! Food of every chaste thought, fountain of all mercy, sum of all purity. Come! Consume in us whatever prevents us from being consumed in you.

St. Mary Magdalene de Pazzi

The Gift Of
Knowledge

Proverbs 8:10:
*Choose my instruction instead
of silver, knowledge rather
than choice gold.*

Dear friends, let us begin our nine-day journey with the Holy Spirit by reflecting on, and praying for the gift of knowledge.

What is the gift of knowledge?

- Knowledge is the gift of the Holy Spirit that makes us more aware of the world that God has made.
- It is the operation of the Holy Spirit opening our minds to understand how things work and fit together.
- It is like being educated by the Holy Spirit, who helps us to build a base of knowledge from which we can operate in the world.

The Holy Spirit communicates knowledge to us in various ways:

- Sometimes he just gives us an answer to a question or a solution to some confusion.
- It could be a clear grasp of how things work and fit together, or it could be an enlightenment about events in the world in which we live.
- Sometimes, the Holy Spirit simply reveals something to us about ourselves, about people, about some secrets.

A good example can be seen in Matthew 16:13-17:

Peter Declares That Jesus Is the Messiah

13 When Jesus came to the region of Caesarea Philippi, He asked His disciples, "Who do people say the Son of Man is?"

14 They replied, "Some say John the Baptist; others say Elijah; and still others, Jeremiah or one of the prophets."

15 "But what about you?" He asked. "Who do you say I am?"

16 Simon Peter answered, "You are the Messiah, the Son of the living God."

17 Jesus replied, "Blessed are you, Simon son of Jonah, for this was not revealed to you by flesh and blood, but by my Father in heaven. Peter was able to come to this awareness by an enlightenment of his mind, even though he did not understand the meaning and implication of Jesus as Christ.

The gift of knowledge is an illumination of our intellect. The Holy Spirit speaks to our Spirit and gives us insight that we are unable to grasp with own limited intelligence.

We also see this at work in the lives of Daniel, Solomon, Stephen, Philip, Paul, Peter and the disciples specifically mentioned in the Acts of the Apostles.

The importance of the gift of knowledge

    I.   Knowledge is important for witnessing to Jesus. Proverbs 19:2 says even zeal is not good without knowledge.
    II.   Knowledge builds our self-confidence and courage.
    III. Knowledge of truth brings joy and happiness to the soul.
    IV. Knowledge liberates us from the assault and risk of ignorance. Knowledge makes us less vulnerable to deceit and manipulation.
    V.   Knowledge gains us respect.

Steps to gaining knowledge

    A. Spend time in prayer, specifically asking for this gift. The more we pray, the more we dispose ourselves to communicate with the Holy Spirit, and to be enlightened by Him.

B. Be resolved to dedicate time to studying more about God and the world around you. Begin to pay more attention and read more, and the Lord will supply His grace upon your effort. In the words of St. Vincent de Paul, "Read some chapter of a devout book....It is very easy and most necessary, for just as you speak to God when at prayer, God speaks to you when you read."

C. Ask questions and engage people who are enlightened and are willing to share. This was how Apollos increased his knowledge with the help of Priscilla and Aquila (Acts 18:26).

D. Do not be afraid to share your opinion and experience. The Holy Spirit communicates knowledge in an atmosphere of sharing.

E. Be humble enough to accept correction in good faith. Sometimes we learn more by being corrected.

Private Reading:
HOSEA 4:6; 6:6; DANIEL 2:21; PHILIPPIANS 3:8

PRAYER FOR KNOWLEDGE

O Holy Spirit of God, I thank you for your work in my life. I come this day to ask that you bestow upon me your gift of knowledge. Make me more aware of the world around me and dispose me to hear your words of wisdom.

Spirit of the living God, speak to my soul, enlighten my mind and help me grasp the important truth necessary for my wellbeing and for the wellbeing of others. May I use this gift to help others and to glorify the name of God, through Christ our Lord.
Amen.

Spirit of knowledge, fall afresh on me

*****

THE GIFT OF
WISDOM

James 1:5, NIV:
*If any of you lacks wisdom, you
should ask God, who gives generously
to all without finding fault, and
it will be given to you.*

Wisdom is another very important gift of the Holy Spirit. It is really related to knowledge, but they are not the same.

- Wisdom is the gift of the Spirit that shows us how to use and apply our knowledge in a given situation. If knowledge is power, wisdom teaches us how to use the power sensibly.
- This gift enables us to act in the best possible way, in every given situation. It helps us to know what is important and what needs to be done.
- Wisdom helps us to make right choices and sensibly handle crisis. This gift is reflected in the way someone lives, talks, relates to others, and conducts his life and affairs.

A good example is King Solomon. Let us read what happened when the queen of Sheba visited him:

I Kings 10:

The Queen of Sheba Visits Solomon

When the queen of Sheba heard about the fame of Solomon and his relationship to the Lord, she came to test Solomon with hard questions. 2 Arriving at Jerusalem with a very great caravan—with camels carrying spices, large quantities of gold, and precious stones—she came to Solomon and talked with him about all that she had on her mind. 3 Solomon answered all her questions; nothing was too hard for the king to explain to her. 4 When the queen of Sheba saw all the wisdom of Solomon and the palace he had built, 5 the food on his table, the seating of his officials, the attending servants in their robes, his cupbearers, and the burnt offerings he made at[a] the temple of the Lord, she was overwhelmed.

The importance of the gift of wisdom

    I. Wisdom enables us to live good, beautiful and sensible lives.

    II. Wisdom saves us from disgrace, error, regret and avoidable crisis.

    III. Wisdom empowers us to help others.

    IV. Wisdom gains us respect from others.

    V. Wisdom gives joy to the one who has it and to others.

Steps to gaining divine wisdom

    A. Wisdom is received through prayers (Read James 1:5, Wisdom 7:7). St. Teresa of Avila said, "You pay God a compliment by asking great things of Him."

    B. Wisdom is gained by learning from our own experiences and from those of others and listening to good advice (Proverbs 19:20).

    C. The greatest place to learn wisdom is in the Bible. When we begin to read and apply what we have read, we become wiser than ever before. Wisdom is not just a book of the Bible; it is also hidden in the pages of the Bible (Psalm 119:98-100; 2 Timothy 3:15-17)

    D. When we try to live rightly in the fear of the Lord and according to His commandments, He bestows His wisdom upon our lives (Read this in Ecclesiastes 2:26, Psalm 111:10).

    E. When we purge our hearts of pride, arrogance, envy, selfishness and hatred (James 3:14-17).

9

Private Reading:
PROVERBS 16:16; WISDOM 9:6; JAMES 3:17

PRAYER FOR WISDOM

O Holy Spirit, thank you for your grace and blessings upon my life. I pray this day for an increase in the gift of Divine wisdom; the wisdom to order my life according to your will; the wisdom to make good decisions; the wisdom to avoid what will lead to regret; the wisdom to handle challenging situations and difficult people; the wisdom to act responsibly in every situation.

O Holy Comforter, this I ask and for this I pray through Jesus the Lord.
Amen.

Spirit of wisdom, fall afresh on me

*****

THE GIFT OF
UNDERSTANDING

Colossians 2:2:
*My goal is that they may be encouraged in heart
and united in love, so that they may have
the full riches of complete understanding,
in order that they may know the
mystery of God, namely, Christ.*

Understanding is another excellent gift of the Holy Spirit.

- Understanding is that gift that helps us to grasp the essence of truth; to know more clearly the mysteries of faith.

- Understanding helps us to see as God sees.

- Understanding is the deepening and the perfection of knowledge. It is a gift of divine insight into a matter; it is not just an awareness but a deeper perception of what we are aware of. It is the opening of the mind. Luke 24:45: *It is a revelation of the deeper meaning of a mystery*.

An example of someone who demonstrated this is Daniel. If we read the book of Daniel, especially from chapters 4 and 5, we see how Daniel was blessed with the understanding of mysteries.

We also see this displayed by the disciples, in the Acts of the Apostles. We see how they came to really grasp the teachings of Jesus and the mysteries of salvation that Christ sought to reveal to them, and how they taught this with accuracy and clarity.

Stephen is also a case study, with his clear grasp and elucidation of the unfolding of the mystery of salvation and its culmination in Christ Jesus (Acts 7).

The scribes and Pharisees knew the scriptures, but they lacked understanding of the meaning. This was why many times, Jesus told them to go and learn the meaning (Matthew 9:9-13; 22:41-46; Mark 12:18-27).

The importance of the gift of understanding

I. Understanding gives us joy and satisfaction.

II. Understanding liberates us from confusion, ignorance and misapplication.

III. We are able to use our understanding to help others deepen their knowledge too.

IV. A person with understanding earns respects and admiration.

V. Understanding makes faith more appreciated, more intelligible, more personal and more credible.

Steps to gaining understanding

A. God promised to give us understanding through prayers (Jeremiah 33:3; 2 Timothy 2:7). In the words of St. Alphonsus Maria de Liguori, "He who prays most, receives most."

B. Through study, especially the Word of God (Psalm 119:130). When we pray and study, we gain not just knowledge, but also understanding.

C. By spending time in silent reflection and meditation. The Lord speaks more to us in this atmosphere.

D. Walking with and relating with people with understanding (Proverbs 13:20).

E. By having the humility to learn from others. Pride impedes understanding.

Private Reading:
PROVERBS 2:6; EPHESIANS 1:17; 1 JOHN 5:20

PRAYER FOR UNDERSTANDING

O Holy Spirit, I come before you today to pray for the gift of understanding. Illuminate my mind; open it to see as you see. Grant me a deeper revelation of your mysteries, and a deeper awareness of truth.

Fill my heart with the joy that comes from understanding and grant me the love and humility to use this gift to serve you and others responsibly.

Amen.

Spirit of understanding, fall afresh on me

*****

THE GIFT OF
COUNSEL

Psalm 32:8:
I will instruct you and teach you the way you should go; I will give you counsel and watch over you.

Counsel is the gift of the Holy Spirit that enables us to make right judgements and give good advice.

- It is the ability to guide and be guided by others, to give and receive good advice, to lead others in doing or choosing what is good and helping them to live rightly.
- The gift of counsel helps us to understand how to respond to difficult situations. It also disposes us to give good advice to others, and to help them understand their situation and cope with their challenges.
- A person with the gift of counsel helps others to identify a problem and work out what can be done to correct it, without manipulating them.

Ahithophel in the Bible had this gift (2 Samuel 16:23), however, he didn't end well. His gift was corrupted by pride and he used it in a wrong context (2 Samuel 17:23).

Joseph used this gift in Egypt, and he was promoted (Genesis 41:33-41).

As we can see from the explanation, the gift of counsel is enhanced by wisdom and understanding.

Jesus Himself is the wonderful counsellor (Isaiah 9:6) and the Holy Spirit which He gives, continues to counsel us and bestow this gift on us.

The importance of the gift of counsel

I. This gift really helps us to serve others and help them to find peace and wholeness.
II. By counsel, we save ourselves and others from making mistakes and regrettable decisions.
III. Counsel gains us respect and admiration.

IV. The gift of counsel helps to promote peace and resolve conflict amicably.

V. Counsel gives joy and fulfilment to the one who has it. There is so much joy in helping someone to successfully deal with a difficult problem.

Steps to obtaining counsel

A. By Praying for it. The Lord wants us to ask Him for what we need, with the confidence of a child approaching a good father. The Lord does not deprive us of anything that is good for us.

B. Attentive listening to the Holy Spirit. To direct others, we must first learn to be directed by the Holy Spirit. We must learn to listen to the Holy Spirit, who speaks to us in different ways: through people, through our thoughts, through pictures, symbols and images, through songs, through our successes and even through our mistakes and failures.

C. Avoid pride, greed and prejudice. These impede the right use of the gift of counsel. We need to set our minds right with God always, in order to be able to obtain and use this gift properly.

D. Study the Word of God. The Word of God enlightens us and helps us to direct our lives and help others too. We need to be open to learning from our experiences, our mistakes and from people's experiences.

Private Reading:
JOB 12:13; PROVERBS 12:15; 24:6; 27:6

PRAYER FOR COUNSEL

O Holy Spirit, one in glory, essence and power with the Father and the Son, you are the teacher, the advocate, the helper, the Spirit of truth promised to us by Jesus.

I humbly ask you to fill my heart with the gift of counsel, so that I may be able to make right judgement in ordering my life, and I may be able to help others in their moment of distress, difficulty and confusion.

Holy Spirit awaken this gift in me for the glory of the name of the Trinity, the growth of the Church, my sanctification and the restoration of peace to others.

Amen.

Spirit of the living God, fall afresh on me.

*****

THE GIFT OF
FORTITUDE

Hebrews 10:36:
*You need to persevere so that
when you have done the will of God,
you will receive what
he has promised*

Fortitude is another word for strength or courage. It refers to spiritual rather than physical strength.

This is the ability to remain faithful and committed to God, no matter the temptations or external forces to the contrary.

- It is the ability to endure suffering and hardship in the practice of the faith.
- Fortitude helps us to put our relationship with God first in our lives, no matter what arises.
- It keeps us going when things are really hard and helps us to keep walking with and holding unto God amidst trials, discouragement, challenges, difficulties.

We see this displayed in people like Noah, prophets like Elijah, in Job, in Joseph, son of Jacob, in the three Hebrew children in the book of Daniel 3, and in the Apostles, after the outpouring of the Holy Spirit.

Job said, *even though He slays me, yet I will trust in Him* (Job 13:15).

It is the gift at work in the lives of the martyrs, who would rather have died than disobey God. It is the gift of endurance.

It strengthens us from giving up or getting discouraged. It makes us endure tough times and difficult people or situations, out of our love for God.

In the words of Pope Francis:

"We all know people who have experienced difficult situations and great suffering. But, think of these men, these women, who lead difficult lives, who struggle to maintain their families, to bring up their children: they do all of this because the spirit of fortitude helps them. ... These brothers and sisters of ours are saints, everyday saints, saints who are concealed among us; they have

the gift of fortitude that allows them to carry out their duties as persons, as fathers, mothers, brothers, sisters and citizens. ... And it is good for us to think about these people: if they do all this, if they can do it, why can't I? it is good for us to ask the Lord for the gift of fortitude."
General audience, May 14, 2014.

The importance of the gift of fortitude

    I. Fortitude is needed to serve God faithfully (Sirach 2:1-9).
    II. Fortitude helps us to overcome obstacles to success (Hebrews 10:39).
    III. Fortitude inspires and encourages others (Hebrews 13:7).
    IV. This gift enables us to have joy and peace in the midst of crises (James 1:2-4).
    V. Fortitude is a powerful way of witnessing to our faith. This was the way the believers in the Acts of the Apostles witnessed to their faith and touched others.

Steps to gaining fortitude

    A. Fortitude is a gift that we receive through prayer. Through earnest prayers, the Lord will not deny us the gift we need to be faithful to Him and bear courageous witness to Him.
    B. By studying and meditating on the heroic examples of saints and martyrs.
    C. Through studying the scriptures. The scriptures help us to grow in our understanding of God. Understanding of God inspires faith and love in us, and faith and love of God strengthen our fidelity to God.
    D. By always contemplating the joy of heaven and the happiness of eternal life. This will help us overcome our fears in life.

E. By sharing our experiences with others and listening to their experiences. We come to understand that we are not alone and that some other people are going through a more difficult time and tougher challenges (1 Peter 5:9).

F.

Private Reading:
MATTHEW 24:13; ROMANS 5:3, 5:4,
2 CORINTHIANS 4:7-9

PRAYER FOR FORTITUDE

O Holy Spirit, I come to you this day, and thank you for all the graces and blessings I have received. I ask you for the gift of fortitude to be able to carry my cross without looking back; to be able to hold firmly unto my faith come what may; to be able to love God above all the attractions of life.

Give me endurance so that I will not give up when things are rough. Help me to persevere to the end and be saved.

Amen.

Spirit of fortitude, fall afresh on me.

*****

THE GIFT OF
FEAR OF THE LORD

Psalm 128:1:
*Blessed are all who
fear the Lord, who walk
in obedience to Him.*

The fear of the Lord is the gift that moves us to recognise the greatness of God and our dependence on Him.

- To fear God does not mean we are scared of Him; rather it suggests awe, reverence, worship, wonder and praise of God, recognising His greatness and love and how much we depend on Him.
- It is a response of love and wonder, rather than a negative emotion.
- Fear of the Lord is that gift that inspires us to obey the Lord faithfully, submit to His discipline, worship Him in awe, and to be very careful to avoid whatever might offend Him, not out of fear of judgement or punishment but out of love for so good a God.
- Anyone who fears the Lord will hate sin and everything that can offend God.

Job is an example of a man who feared God. See how he was introduced in the Bible:

In the land of Uz there lived a man whose name was Job. This man was blameless and upright; he feared God and shunned evil (Job 1:1).

St. Thomas says it is fear of separating oneself from God.

In the words of St. Bonaventure: "Qui Deum timet, securus est ubique." "He who fears God, remains firmly secure in Him."

The importance of the gift of fear of the Lord

1. The fear of the Lord is wisdom. There is no wisdom without first understanding who God is and having reverence for Him (Proverbs 1:7).

II. The fear of the Lord brings blessings, as in the case of Joseph. God is honoured by those who fear Him (Psalm 115:13; 145:19, 128).

III. The fear of the Lord gains us people's trust, love and respect. It also frees us from fear of people (Daniel 3:16-18, 28-29, Matthew 10:28).

IV. The fear of God discourages us from the enticement of sin and so liberates us from the slavery into which we are plunged by sin (Psalm 119:45, Proverbs 16:6, John 8:34).

V. Fear of God, even though not prompted by dread of punishment, saves us from being punished (Ecclesiastes 8:12-13; Proverbs 28:14).

Steps to obtaining fear of the Lord

A. It is principally to be sought through prayer. Through prayers we can obtain from God anything that does not jeopardise our salvation.

B. Study the Word of God and pray for understanding. When we understand the scriptures, we become aware of God's greatness, power and goodness. This awareness leads us to awe.

C. Always think about God's goodness in your life and remember how He has manifested His greatness in times past (Psalm 77:11-12, Psalm 103:2). Recalling God's goodness, teaches us to love and trust Him and avoid what offends His goodness.

D. Be careful of your company and those you mingle with. When we mingle with people who are God fearing, we begin to learn their ways; when we mingle with people who have no reverence for God, they influence us (1 Corinthians 15:33).

E. Always think about the day you will stand face to face before God. Remember when you will render account of your life, remember when your eternal destiny will be decided (Sirach 7:36).

Private Reading:
PROVERBS 14:27; 19:23, 22:4; 1 PETER 2:17; JOB 28:28

PRAYER FOR FEAR OF THE LORD

O most Holy Spirit, you are the giver of all good gifts. Instil in me the fear of God. Help me to love God above all things, to come before Him with awe, reverence and worship. Help me hate whatever offends His goodness.

Let me ponder every day on His goodness in my life and love Him with the whole of my being. May nothing ever separate me from a God who is so great, so good and so loving to me.

Amen.

Spirit of the living God, fall afresh on me.

*****

THE GIFT OF
PIETY

Psalm 100:2:
Serve the LORD with gladness!
Come into his presence
with singing!

This gift is very important in our society today. Many people worship God as if out of compulsion or coercion, as if fulfilling an undesirable obligation. Many people find religion too burdensome and a deprivation of their freedom.

Many people come to Church and their discomfort in God's presence is so evident.

This is not how it is meant to be. We ought to worship God with delight, with enthusiasm. Praying to God ought to be something sweet and joyful. Coming to His presence is supposed to fill us with rejoicing; being in His presence is supposed to be satisfying and enjoyable.

God does not want us to worship Him just out of sense of duty, but as a response of joy prompted by love. This is what piety does.

- It makes us hunger for God; it makes us want more of Him.
- Piety creates a willingness in us, a gravitation towards God.
- It makes the practise of religion sweet and desirable. It is the gift of devotion.
-

When someone has the gift of piety, he/she needs no one to beg him/her to pray. He/she does not find worship boring or unexciting. He/she does not complain of time spent in God's presence. My experience is that piety makes one a God-addict in a very sweet way.

Piety helps us to devoutly fulfil religious obligations.

Do you know someone who loves to pray so much, who spend hours in prayers? Someone who joyfully prays as many times as possible in a day? Someone who just wants to talk about God and longs to be in His presence?

This is someone with the gift of piety.

Like the Psalmist in Psalm 122:

I rejoiced with those who said to me, "Let us go to the house of the LORD."

And the prophecy of Isaiah:

Many peoples will come and say, "Come, let us go up to the mountain of the LORD, to the temple of the God of Jacob. He will teach us His ways, so that we may walk in His paths" (Isaiah 2:3).

The importance of the gift of piety

I.   Piety makes the practise of religion sweeter and livelier. It is the life of religious practices. It animates spirituality.

II. Piety enables us to find joy and peace in God in the midst of challenges around.

III. Piety inspires others and it stirs faith in them.

IV. The gift of piety disposes us to receiving other gifts and fruits of the Holy Spirit, such as joy, peace, faith, kindness, goodness, self-control, understanding, fortitude, wisdom, knowledge, counsel and so on.

V.   Someone with the gift of piety mediates and ministers God's power, blessing and mercy to others.

Steps to receiving piety

A. Praying for it with persistence and faith (Hebrews 11:1).

B. Associating with those who have it. Piety ignites something in others. When you move close to a pious person, you begin to feel challenged by their devotion and before you know it, something is happening in your life as well.

C. Meditating on the life and examples of Holy men and women. We are easily drawn by the heroic examples of saints and they inspire us to imitate their spiritual excellence.
(Hebrews 13:7).

D. Intentionally detaching ourselves from things that compete with God for our attention and affection. Many people are not progressing spiritually due to distraction; they have lost the sweetness of being in God's presence because other things are competing for their time and attention. Lack of restraint in our use of social media is one greatest obstacles to piety.

E. Joining groups in the Church that can help you to grow spiritually; groups of those who worship God joyfully, who are attentive to the Holy Spirit and seek to help one another grow.

Private Reading:
PSALM 16:11; 43:4; COLOSSIANS 3:23

PRAYER FOR PIETY

O great Comforter, you are co-creator, co-eternal and co-redeemer with the Father and the Son. I worship your majesty. I call upon you Holy Spirit to bestow upon me the gift of piety, so that henceforth I may love God more, honour Him more, serve Him more joyfully, surrender to Him more totally, pray to Him more fervently and enjoy His love more graciously.

May I never cease to find delight and happiness in serving God and may I forever find joy and fulfilment in His presence.

Amen.

Spirit of piety, fall afresh on me.

*****

Growing in Intimacy
With The Holy Spirit

Ephesians 1:13-14:
13 And you also were included in Christ when you heard the message of truth, the gospel of your salvation. When you believed, you were marked in Him with a seal, the promised Holy Spirit, 14 who is a deposit guaranteeing our inheritance until the redemption of those who are God's possession—to the praise of His glory.

The Holy Spirit is the gift of the Father, through the Son, to all of us who are children of God. He has been given to us to be our helper.

We are expected to establish a deep communion, a dynamic rapport, a fruitful friendship and lively intimacy with the Paraclete. This is what St. Paul meant when he prayed in I Corinthians 13:13 for the communion or fellowship of the Holy Spirit to be with us.

The Holy Spirit wants to be our friend; He yearns to be wanted; He waits to be welcomed and desires to be hosted.

How do I grow in intimacy with the spirit?

I.   *Pray for it.*
     We need to ask God in faith and constancy, for a greater intimacy with the Holy Spirit.
     Read Luke 11:9-13 New International Version (NIV).

II. *Spend more time in God's presence.*
     Every friendship demands time and communication to grow. It is the same for friendship with the Holy Spirit. We need to be able to set time aside to just be in God's presence, to be "in the atmosphere."

     Most of us are so busy; we have families, jobs, kids to look after, projects, meetings and some willed distractions here and there. We have many things that require daily time and attention and so we do not have time to place ourselves in God's presence, where we can commune with the Holy Spirit.

     We need to be more resolved and disciplined. We need this intimacy with the Spirit in our lives.

34

III.   *Study more about the Holy Spirit and His works in our lives.*

There is also an intellectual dimension to growing in intimacy with the Holy Spirit. In any relationship we need to keep knowing the other person. Knowledge of our friends, their characters and personalities will help us to relate with them better.

We need to study more about the person of the Holy Spirit and ways He is working in the lives of people. Often, we don't really like to read, but we need to shake off our mental lethargy and inertia and search for knowledge and understanding of the Spirit.

In the scriptures we can learn so much about the operations, manifestations and attributes of the Holy Spirit, especially in the Acts of the Apostles, where we see how the early Christians lived in, walked with, were led by and were attentive to the Holy Spirit.

I recommend the book of the Acts of the Apostles to us all. If we have read this before we can read again. The word of God is ever new, alive and active.

IV.   *Relate to Him naturally as a teacher, comforter, guide, prayer partner, a revealer of Gods purpose, counsellor, and a helper.*

Learn to talk to the Holy Spirit. Converse with him, share your concerns, ask questions, seek clarification, open your hearts, talk about your burdens. Talk to the Holy Spirit as a supernatural friend who is ever at your side; that is the meaning of Advocate (called to be at one's side).

I got this very interesting and warm passage from the official handbook of the Legion of Mary.

"The Holy Spirit is Love, Beauty, Power, Wisdom, Purity, and all else that is of God. If He descends in plentitude, every need can be met, and the most grievous problem can be brought into conformity with the Divine Will."

The handbook tells us one of the conditions for growing in the Holy Spirit:

"The man who thus makes the Holy Spirit his helper (Ps. 77) enters into the tide of omnipotence...One of the conditions ..... is that we appreciate the Holy Spirit Himself as a real, distinct, Divine Person with His appropriate mission in regard to us. This appreciation of Him will not be maintained, except there be a reasonably frequent turning of the mind to Him."

The official handbook of the Legion of Mary (1993), chapter 7, The Legionary and the Holy Trinity.

V. *Make an effort to be faithful to God by avoiding whatever offends God and can grieve the Holy Spirit.*

Whenever we have done anything wrong or the Spirit convicts us of any sin, we need to immediately seek forgiveness from God. We need to constantly show that we cherish our relationship with God, and that we want to avoid whatever can ruin that.

I want to specifically mention here five sins that we need to constantly watch out for, so that they don't impede our relationship with the Holy Spirit.

36

- Lust or unchastity
- Pride
- Envy
- Unforgiveness
- Laziness.

VI.   *Have passion and care for souls.*

Souls matter to the Holy Spirit; the more we are zealous about the conversion of souls, the more we dispose ourselves to the Holy Spirit to use us. His power is not to make us rich or famous, but to make God known and to bring as many people as possible to the kingdom of grace. St. Rose of Lima said, "Know that the greatest service that man can offer to God is to help convert souls."

VII.   *Use the gifts and do not resist.*

When the Holy Spirit has given us gifts, He wants us to use them as directed and moved. The Holy Spirit does not want us to be resistant to Him and His prompting. Sometimes we may feel the Holy Spirit moving us to help someone, say something to someone, pray for someone, advise someone, and we should not resist the impulse. The more we are obedient to the Holy Spirit's prompting, the more He uses us and relates with us. In this case we need discernment to distinguish between what the Holy Spirit is saying and what we are thinking or imagining.

VIII. *Closeness to our Blessed Mother*

The handbook of the Legion of Mary has it that "Every devotion to the Blessed Virgin can be made a wide-open way to the Holy Spirit."

When we intentionally draw close to our Blessed Mother and develop an intimacy with her, we begin to feel the nearness of the Holy Spirit too, as in the case of Elizabeth when Mary entered her house (Luke 1:41).

Saint Louis de Montfort enthusiastically asserts: "Those who love Mary, the Holy Spirit flings Himself into their souls."

Mary is the Daughter of God the Father, the Mother of God the Son, and Mary is the Mystical Spouse of the Holy Spirit. To love the Blessed Virgin Mary is to open a floodgate of graces and the powerful invasion of the Holy Spirit in our lives.

PRAYER FOR AN INTIMACY WITH THE HOLY SPIRIT

O Holy Spirit, the bond of love between the Father and the Son, you are the finger of God and the sweet guest of my soul.

I welcome you O Holy Spirit; come and renew me, come and revive me, come and rekindle in me the fire of divine love, and make me grow in intimacy with you. Make me more attentive to your prompting, more docile to your instruction, more aware of your presence. May I grow in my relationship with you and find in you always, a sweet companion, a faithful friend, a worthy counsellor and the wisest teacher. Speak always to the depth of my soul and move me to respond with joy, love and obedience.

Amen.

Assignment:
Study the Acts of the Apostles, paying closer attention to what the Holy Spirit did in, with and through the believers.
Pray for a dynamic personal experience too.

Spirit of the living God, fall afresh on me

*****

BEING ATTENTIVE TO
THE HOLY SPIRIT

John 14:26:
But the Advocate, the Holy Spirit, whom the Father will send in my name, will teach you all things and will remind you of everything I have said to you.

Through baptism and confirmation, we have all received the Holy Spirit. However, we are called daily to foster communion with the Holy Spirit. The Holy Spirit does not just fill us and abide with us, He wants to teach us, remind us, explain things to us, instruct us and inspire us.

I wish to cite here the example of Simeon who is a paradigm of what it means to be attentive to the Holy Spirit. Luke 2:25 says he was a righteous and devout man and the Holy Spirit was upon him. Verse 26 says it had been revealed to him by the Holy Spirit, that he should not see death before he had seen the Lord's Christ. Verse 27 says:

And inspired by the Spirit, he came into the temple; and when the parents brought in the child Jesus....

We see three things in Simeon:

- He was filled with the Spirit.
- He was attentive to the Spirit.
- He responded to the Spirit.

Like Simeon, the Holy Spirit wants to communicate with us. We see so much of this in the Acts of the Apostles; how the Holy Spirit ordered, guided and directed the activities of the early Church.

The Holy Spirit still speaks today. We need to be attentive. The Spirit tries to speak to us or get our attention through many different means.

Today, let us reflect on some means through which the Holy Spirit tries to speak to us.

I. Symbols:

Sometimes the Holy Spirit communicates to us by using symbols, pictures or images.

This can happen when we are meditating or in an atmosphere of prayer. Sometimes we just see through our minds, images or pictures communicating a message to us. We do not need to force ourselves to create an image, the Holy Spirit just presents them to us, and it is so clear and vivid. These images communicate important messages.

A good example of this is in Acts 10:9-16, when Peter saw all kinds of animals in a great sheet.

Whenever the Holy Spirit reveals something through symbols or pictures, He also helps us to understand the revelation.

II. Speaks directly to our Spirit through thoughts, impressions, ideas.

Through this, the Holy Spirit can give us insight, words of knowledge, prophetic insight, clarity, or inspiration.

III. Illumination of the mind, especially to understand a mystery, a Bible passage.

Personally, I hear the voice of the Holy Spirit more when I am studying or meditating on the Word of God. Whenever we invite the Holy Spirit to explain the Word of God to us, we experience Him in a new way and the experience is so joyful. Just think of Philip and the Ethiopian eunuch in Acts 8:26-40; that is exactly what the Holy Spirit does for us. He unlocks our mind and enlightens it to comprehend the sweet and saving truth of the Word of God.

We must cultivate the habit of studying the Bible, not just for information but for transformation. This is by asking God to change our lives through what we read. The Holy Spirit is the principal author of the Scriptures. In fact, the Bible is the intention of the Holy Spirit written down by human authors and so, the Holy Spirit Himself is the best interpreter of His intention.

IV. Through other people.

Many times, the Holy Spirit speaks to us through other people. Here again, we need real discernment.

With some of the books I have recently written, the suggestions came from other people and I could sense clearly in my Spirit, that the Holy Spirit was speaking through them to me. I guess the Holy Spirit knew I probably would have rationalised the thoughts and possibly debunked them.

Sometimes the Spirit speaks to us through advice, counsel, corrections or in our discussion with others. Someone may just say something that speaks directly to our situation.

At other times, it may be through a preaching, which addresses our exact experience. The Holy Spirit also ministers to us through songs

Sometimes we are struggling with something or pondering whether to do something or not, or we just have some unanswered questions in our mind and then, on coming for Mass, the homily of that day touches exactly our situation.

All those deeply improbable coincidences are usually driven by the Holy Spirit.

V.   Through our challenges and troubles.
Sometimes we become more attentive when we are sober and broken. The Holy Spirit often communicates to us through the challenges of our lives, through our darkness, through closed doors.

This may be through an experience of losing a job, failing a test, an unsuccessful interview, through the breakdown of a relationship after doing everything to keep it, sometimes through the crisis we face in our vocation, or through some strange circumstances we find ourselves in. In all these, we must always learn to ask, "Holy Spirit, what do you want me to learn from this." God has something to teach us through whatever happens to us, but we must know how to listen.

It is written in Revelations 2:29:

Anyone with ears to hear must listen to the Spirit and understand what he is saying to the Churches.

VI.   Through dreams and visions.

We read in Joel 2:28-29:
And afterward, I will pour out my Spirit on all people. Your sons and daughters will prophesy, your old men will dream dreams, your young men will see visions. Even on my servants, both men and women, I will pour out my Spirit in those days.
(Read also Numbers 12:6)

The Bible is replete with examples of people whom God communicated with through dreams and visions.

God still communicates with us through dreams and visions. I must say that it is not every dream that is meaningful. I see many people panic about every dream. They want to make sense of every dream. I am an expert in having meaningless dreams.

However, I have also received vivid and direct messages from the Holy Spirit through dreams.

Dreams by the Holy Spirit are remembered, they are vivid, they do not fade, they linger longer in our minds, unlike some dreams that are quickly forgotten or meaningless. When the Holy Spirit communicates through dreams, He helps us to understand or arranges someone to help us understand. The Holy Spirit will not communicate something to us and not see to it that we understand.

In conclusion, we can never exhaust the means by which the Holy Spirit communicates with us; He moves, blows and operates as He wills, because He is God. However, we need to be constantly attentive to these and other various means with which the Holy Spirit wants to speak to us.

We may need to be still and free our minds of worries, fears, hatred, prejudice and bitterness, so that we can hear more clearly the sweet voice of the comforter (Psalm 46:10).

PRAYER FOR GREATER ATTENTIVENESS

Most Holy Spirit, you are a wonderful gift of God to humanity. Our lives would be vain, empty and dry without you.

I call upon you today to make me more attentive to you, dispose me to hear and heed your message, rid me of my deafness and inattentiveness, grant me docility, openness and greater sensitivity.

May your voice bring joy to my life and the lives of others and lead me to fulfilling God's purpose for my life.

Amen.

Spirit of the living God, fall afresh on me

*****

Prayers for the Fruits of the Holy Spirit.

O Holy Spirit of God, the third person of the Most Holy Trinity, I thank you for the work of renewal and sanctification you are doing in my life.

I pray today for a re-filling and re-awakening of your divine attributes in me. I want you to bring to life in me again your fruits which are the effects of your presence in me.

Give me **love** that I may love you above all else and to love others genuinely and sacrificially for your sake.

Give me **joy** O Lord, so that no matter the circumstances around me, I will continue to be glad and grateful to you.

Grant me **patience** that I may patiently wait for the fulfilment of your promises in my life.

O Holy Spirit fill my heart with **peace** that I may rest tranquil and undisturbed even in the midst of uncertainties.

Make me genuinely **kind** to everyone I relate with, that I may treat them with respect and charity.

I ask for the manifestation of the fruit of **goodness**, that I may be motivated to do what is good, right and just, always.

I pray that you make me **faithful** to you and in my relationship with others.

O Holy Spirit endow me with something of your **gentleness**, so that I may attend to every person and issue with a divine calmness and reasonableness.

I ask you for **self-control** so that I may keep my desires under check.

Make my life **modest**, orderly and free of pride or self-exaltation. Lord, I am in dire need of **longanimity** that I may patiently bear with difficult people and situations without acting harshly, rashly or in a manner contrary to faith and reason.

I pray today for **chastity** so that my words, thoughts and deeds may be free of all impurity defilement.

Thank you Holy Spirit, because I have asked in faith and I believe that I shall receive in abundant measures through Jesus Christ our Lord.

Amen.

*****

Prayers for the Seven Gifts of the Holy Spirit.

O Holy Spirit, I thank you for your work in my life; your work of renewal, sanctification and revival. I open myself to you O Holy Spirit; fan into flames, your gifts which I received when I was baptised and confirmed.

Refill me with the gift of **knowledge** so that I may become more aware of my environment and gain insights that surpass the limit of my intellect.

Let your **wisdom** be upon my life so that I may make the right choices and decisions in life, and handle issues with greater poise, care and prudence.

I pray for **understanding**, so that I grasp better the mysteries of my salvation, to gain more clarity about matters and to see what God is trying to show me.

I need O Lord, a reawakening of the gift of **counsel** so that I may make right judgement and help others to do the same.

Grant to me O Holy Spirit, the grace of **fortitude**, so that I may endure difficulties and hardships with greater patience and joyful submission to God's will.

Lord, may I always think of you and honour you with **awe and reverence** and be careful to avoid whatever offends your love for me.

Fill my soul with **piety**, so that I hunger and yearn more for you every day and serve you with utmost delight and joy.

This I ask and for these I pray, trusting in the promise of God the Father through His Son, Our Lord Jesus Christ, in union with you, O Holy Spirit.
Amen.

*****

Prayer for a greater attentiveness to the Holy Spirit.

O Holy Spirit of God, you are always seeking to teach me, enlighten, direct and inspire me. I pray that you will dispose me to listen more to you, to hear when you speak, to understand when you communicate, to obey when you direct, to follow when you lead, to do what you instruct and to refrain from what you detest. May I live each day in a greater attentiveness to you. Amen.

*****

Prayer to grow in intimacy with the Holy Spirit.

Most Holy Spirit, gift of God the Father and the Son, co-equal, co-divine, co-eternal; you eternally proceed from the Father and the Son and together with them you are adored and glorified. Without your aid, it is impossible to live a worthy and fruitful Christian life. I desire to grow in intimacy with you. I want to become more aware of your presence and power, more attentive to your call. I wish to grow in my understanding of who you are, and I want to surrender myself to you as a vessel. I want you to use me to touch lives and save souls for the glory of your name. Thank you O Holy Spirit; I worship you as God together with the Father and the Son, now and forever.
Amen.

*****

Prayer for the manifestation of the Holy Spirit.

O Holy Spirit, you are the first fruit of Christ's ascension, and the fulfilment of His promise to ever remain with us and in us. You are the helper sent to be with us; you are the giver of gifts and graces.

I pray today for a greater and fuller manifestation of your presence in my life. I empty myself; fill me, fill me with your love, your graces, your power, your holiness, your gifts, your attributes and endowments. I surrender to you to use me as a vessel of your glory. Anoint me with your power, minister to others through me for your glory and the sanctification of souls. Amen.

*****

Prayer for an experience of the power of the Holy Spirit

Come Holy Spirit, fill the hearts of your faithful, and enkindle in them the fire of your love.

Send forth your Spirit and they shall be created, and You shall renew the face of the earth.

Lord Jesus, before ascending to heaven, you promised to send your Holy Spirit upon your disciples and all who believe in you. On the day of Pentecost, you fulfilled your promise to them, and 'til this day you have continued to send your Holy Spirit to fill the hearts of your faithful. I humbly pray that you renew in me the Holy Spirit whom I received at my baptism. I pray for a greater experience of the presence and the power of the Holy Spirit. Let your Spirit O Lord, come and transform my weakness to strength. Let Him be my teacher, my advocate, my friend, my comforter.

Lord, as in the days of the Apostles, I invite the Holy Spirit to come upon me afresh, so that my life henceforth will be lived under the impulse and unction of the third person of the Trinity. Amen.

Spirit of the Living God fall afresh on me.

Private Reading: Joel 2:28-29

*****

EPILOGUE

I hope this nine-day journey has been meaningful and impactful. Let us claim in faith the gifts of the Holy Spirit. We also pray for a greater attentiveness to the Holy Spirit.

I urge you to look forward to series two on the fruits of the Holy Spirit, and series three on the manifestations of the Holy Spirit.

May I close this reflective journey by repeating this prayer of St. Paul to the Colossians which I feel draws all of our discourses together:

...We continually ask God to fill you with the knowledge of His will, through all the wisdom and understanding that the Spirit gives, so that you may live a life worthy of the Lord and please Him in every way: bearing fruit in every good work, growing in the knowledge of God, being strengthened with all power according to His glorious might so that you may have great endurance and patience, and giving joyful thanks to the Father, who has qualified you to share in the inheritance of His holy people in the kingdom of light.
(Colossians 1:9-12).

*****

SOURCES

The Holy Bible, Revised Standard Version, second Catholic Edition, Ignatian Press, San Francisco, 2006.

New International Version (NIV) Holy Bible, New International Version®, NIV® Copyright ©1973, 1978, 1984, 2011 by Biblica.Inc.

Calder, Helen. 7 ways to grow in intimacy with the Holy Spirit, 2015, enlivenpublishing.com.

Chapman, Geoffrey. Catechism of the Catholic Church, Cassel and Co, London, England: 1995.

Deibert, Brannon. What are the gifts of the Holy Spirit? 2019, christianity.com.

Dias-Pabon, Luis Angel. Who is the Holy Spirit. Csb Fisher of Men Bible, August, 2019, biblestudytools.com.

Hertzenberg, Stephanie. 5 Ways the Holy Spirit tries to try your attention, 2020, beliefnet.com.

Kosloski, Philip. What are the seven gifts of the Holy Spirit? 2017, aleteia.org.

Kovacik, Gary. Catholic Saints, pinterest.com

Inspiring quotes, mycatholic.life

Noyes, Penny. What are the fruits of the Spirit? 2019, christianity.com.

Savchuk, Vladimir. 5 steps to deeper relationship with the Holy Spirit, 2018, hungrygen.com

ThoughtCo. "The Seven Gifts of the Holy Spirit." Learn Religions, 2020, learnreligions.com.

Saints quotes on prayers, whitelilyoftrinity.com

*****

BOOKS BY THE SAME AUTHOR

He Sent Forth His Word, Series 1: Homilies for Sundays, Year A
.

He Sent Forth His Word, Series 2: Homilies for Sundays, Year B.

He Sent Forth His Word, Series 3: Homilies for Sundays, Year C.

He Sent Forth His Word, Series 4: Homilies for the Liturgical Seasons of Advent, Christmas, Lent and Easter.

He Sent Forth His Word, Series 5: Homilies for Feasts and Solemnities.

He Sent Forth His Word, Series 6: Homilies for Weekdays, Cycle I.

He Sent Forth His Word, Series 7: Homilies for Weekdays, Cycle II.

A Light to My Path: A Collection of Retreat Talks and Reflections.

His Voice Goes Forth: A Collection of Vocal Meditations and Nuggets.

Lord, Teach Us to Pray: Prayers for Various Occasions.

Seven Days Journey with the Lord: A Handbook for a Self-facilitated Retreat.

Praying with the Psalms.

What God has Joined Together: A Handbook for Marriage Preparation Course.

Whom Shall I Send: A Seven-day Journey with the Lord through His Word.

They Shall be Called My Children: Reflections and Prayers for Children.

When the Spirit Comes Upon You, Series 2:
A Twelve-day Reflection and Prayers for the Fruits of the Holy Spirit.

When the Spirit Comes Upon You, Series 3:
A Nine-day Reflection and Prayers for the Manifestation of the Holy Spirit.

*****

Printed in Great Britain
by Amazon

46164849R00047